TRIBES of NATIVE AMERICA

Shoshone

edited by Marla Felkins Ryan
and Linda Schmittroth

BLACKBIRCH®
PRESS

THOMSON
——✦——™
GALE

San Diego • Detroit • New York • San Francisco • Cleveland
New Haven, Conn. • Waterville, Maine • London • Munich

THOMSON

————★————

GALE

For more information, contact
The Gale Group, Inc.
27500 Drake Rd.
Farmington Hills, MI 48331-3535
Or you can visit our Internet site at http://www.gale.com

LIBRARY OF CONGRESS CATALOGING-IN-PUBLICATION DATA

Shoshone / Marla Felkins Ryan, book editor; Linda Schmittroth, book editor.
    v. cm. — (Tribes of Native America)
Includes bibliographical references.
Contents: Shoshone name — Origins and group affiliations — History — Shoshone
resistance — Daily life — War rituals — Current tribal issues.
    ISBN 1-56711-722-8 (alk. paper)
    1. Shoshoni Indians—Juvenile literature. [1. Shoshoni Indians. 2. Indians of North
America—Great Basin.] I. Ryan, Marla Felkins. II. Schmittroth, Linda. III. Series.

E99.S4 S46 2003
979.004'9745—dc21

2002015829

Printed in United States
10 9 8 7 6 5 4 3 2 1

Table of Contents

SHOSHONE

Name

Shoshone (pronounced *shuh-SHOW-nee*), or Shoshoni. The name may mean "high-growing grass." The Shoshone call themselves by several names that mean "people." Others often called them "snake people," for two reasons. First, they lived near the Snake River. Second, in battle, warriors carried rattles that looked like snakes.

The Shoshone are known by many names, including "snake people."

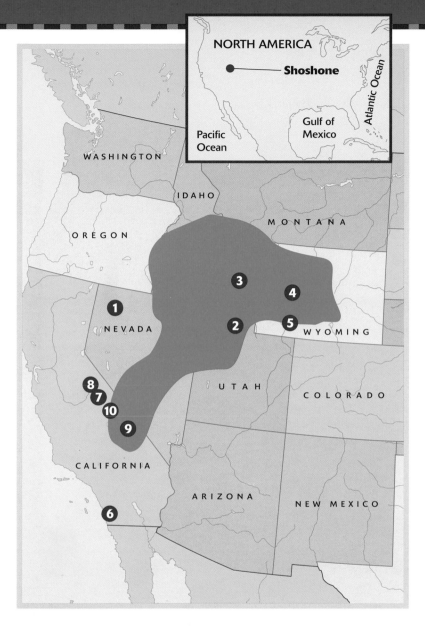

NORTH AMERICA

Shoshone

Pacific Ocean

Gulf of Mexico

Atlantic Ocean

WASHINGTON

IDAHO

MONTANA

OREGON

NEVADA

WYOMING

UTAH

COLORADO

CALIFORNIA

ARIZONA

NEW MEXICO

Shoshone Contemporary Communities

1. Twelve Shoshone communities
2. Northeastern Band of Shoshone Indians
3. Northwestern Band of Shoshone Nation, Utah and Idaho
4. Eastern Shoshone Tribe
5. Northwestern Band of Shoshone Nation, Wyoming
6. Atahun Shoshone of San Juan Capistrano
7. Big Pine Band of Paiute Shoshone Indians
8. Bishop Reservation
9. Death Valley Timbi-Sha Shoshone Band
10. Lone Pine Reservation

Shaded areas: Traditional lands of the Shoshone in present-day Idaho, Nevada, Utah, Wyoming, California, Oregon, and Montana.

Where are the traditional Shoshone lands?

The Shoshone once lived in parts of California, Oregon, Nevada, Idaho, Utah, and Wyoming. Today, they live on or near reservations on their former lands.

What has happened to the population?

In 1845, there were about 4,500 Northern and Western Shoshone. In a 1990 population count by the U.S. Census Bureau, 9,506 people said they were Shoshone. Most lived in Wyoming (1,752), Idaho (676), Nevada (2,637), and California (1,595).

Some early Shoshone lived near the Snake River (pictured) in Idaho. Today, most live on reservations in the western United States.

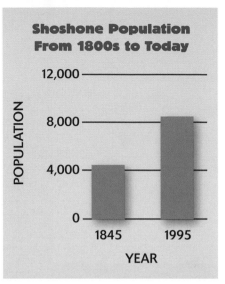

Shoshone Population From 1800s to Today

POPULATION

12,000

8,000

4,000

0

1845   1995

YEAR

Origins and group ties

Early Shoshone probably moved north from the Southwest between about A.D. 1 and A.D. 1000. After that, many Shoshone groups, or bands, lived in the Great Basin, between the Rocky Mountains and the Sierra Nevadas. Some Shoshone groups have ties to the Paiute, Comanche, and Ute tribes.

The Shoshone may be best known because Sacajawea (pronounced *sak-uh-juh-WEE-uh;* also spelled "Sacagawea"), who guided the Lewis and Clark expedition, was part of the tribe. At first, the Shoshone were friendly with white settlers. This changed as they were forced to live on reservations. Today, they still struggle to win rights to their old lands.

The Great Basin area was home to many Shoshone after they moved from the Southwest.

HISTORY

The Northern and Eastern groups became wanderers who hunted and gathered where food was plentiful. They also began to hunt buffalo. This was easier after they got horses late in the 17th century. The tribe soon had conflicts with other buffalo-hunting tribes, such as the Blackfeet and Arapaho. These problems, along with a 1782 smallpox epidemic, led the Eastern Shoshone to move to Wyoming.

Left: Explorers Meriwether Lewis and William Clark were among the first whites the Shoshone met. Below: Many Shoshone hunted buffalo for food.

• Timeline •

1607
English colonists settle Jamestown, Virginia

1620
Mayflower lands at Plymouth, Massachusetts

c. 1700
The Northern and Eastern Shoshone get horses and become buffalo hunters

1776
America declares independence from England

1782
The Eastern Shoshone suffer a smallpox outbreak and attacks by the Blackfeet

1805
The Shoshone meet Lewis and Clark

1861
American Civil War begins

January 1863
The Bear River Massacre occurs

Sacajawea was a Shoshone woman who helped guide explorers Lewis and Clark on their western expedition.

Shoshone help American explorers and settlers

In the 1500s, the Shoshone first saw Spanish settlers. Later, they met other explorers. Still, they had little contact with foreigners. Their relations with whites really began with the 1804–1806 Lewis and Clark expedition. The explorers met a Shoshone when they hired fur trapper Toussaint Charbonneau to be their interpreter. Charbonneau's Shoshone wife, Sacajawea, became the expedition's most important guide. With her help, Lewis and Clark made their way from the Missouri River to the Pacific Ocean.

American settlers came to the West soon after Lewis and Clark mapped the region. Pioneers, trappers, and traders began to press onto Shoshone lands. The Mormons, a religious group, came too. They founded Salt Lake City,

1863
The first Treaty of Fort Bridger is signed. It sets aside reservation land for Shoshone groups

1865
Civil War ends

1868
The second Treaty of Fort Bridger is signed. It reduces the amount of reservation lands

1900
Chief Washakie dies

1914–1918
WWI fought in Europe

1930s
Shoshone bands form tribal governments

1941
Bombing at Pearl Harbor forces United States into WWII

1945
WWII ends.

1950s
Reservations no longer controlled by federal government

1990s and after
Struggles over land rights go on. Reparations Act brings about the return of burial remains to native tribes

Utah, in 1847. The lure of gold in California sent more whites west in 1849. So did the discovery of silver in Nevada in 1857. This westward movement changed the lives of the Shoshone forever.

Shoshone resistance

The Shoshone resisted white settlement in the early 1860s. Indian war parties attacked wagon trains, mail carriers, and telegraph crews. The Shoshone were upset partly because whites hunted so many buffalo that the herds began to disappear. To keep Americans safe from Indian raids, Fort Douglas was built near Salt Lake City. In January 1863, three hundred army troops went on a raid to punish Chief Bear Hunter and his Northern Shoshone at their village, 140 miles away.

The Indians built barricades to be ready for the soldiers' arrival. The Shoshone had never felt the full force of the U.S. Army, though. Gunfire exploded in the village on January 29. In four hours, the troops killed 250 Shoshone, ruined seventy homes, and took 175 horses. Only fourteen whites were killed and forty-nine injured.

Northern and Eastern Shoshone make peace

The Northern and Eastern Shoshone were ready to make peace after the Bear River Massacre. Later in 1863, Shoshone chiefs signed the first of several treaties. They agreed to sell land to the U.S. government, but the payments were rarely made. The government began to send all American Indians to reservations. Many Shoshone did not want to move. As time went on, though, they had no choice. Eventually, all the Northern Shoshone were moved to the Fort Hall Reservation in eastern Idaho.

By the start of the 20th century, most Northern Shoshone lived at Fort Hall. As timber businesses, railroad companies, and miners came, Shoshone lands were reduced from 1.8 million acres to 544,000 acres.

In the early 1900s, these Shoshone men in traditional dress took part in a fair near Fort Hall, Idaho. Most Northern Shoshone were forced by the U.S. government to live on the reservation there at that time.

The Wind River Reservation was set up for the Eastern Shoshone in 1863 on 44 million acres in Wyoming. After about five years, a new treaty made that area less than 2.8 million acres. The Eastern Shoshone did not break their peace with the Americans, however. In fact, under Chief Washakie's leadership, they helped the Americans fight the Sioux in the 1870s. The Shoshone felt betrayed when the government moved the Shoshone's old enemies, the Arapaho, to the Wyoming reservation in 1878.

Chief Washakie
(center) was
leader of the
Eastern Shoshone
until 1900.

After the death of Washakie in 1900, the Eastern
Shoshone faced one tragedy after another. They
suffered starvation and outbreaks of measles and
tuberculosis (a very contagious disease that usually
attacks the lungs). The population fell greatly.

Western Shoshone

The Western Shoshone signed the Treaty of Ruby
Valley in 1863. They agreed to let settlers set up
businesses on their land. They also said they would
stop their roaming life. They promised to move to
reservations later. They did not, however, agree to
give up their lands.

In the early decades of the 20th century, many
Western Shoshone tried to avoid the move to
reservations. The U.S. government agreed to found
colonies (small Indian settlements) in Nevada. The
Shoshone could live there or on reservations. By

1927, only about half of the Western Shoshone lived on reservations.

Shoshone in the 20th century and beyond

In the 1930s, the Shoshone went through some positive changes. They were able to have some self-government. Their quality of life also improved. They began to share their culture with whites. At the same time, they worked hard to hold on to their culture. They taught and used the Shoshone language. They built schools and cultural centers. They also held powwows (song-and-dance celebrations).

The Shoshone people live on or near eighteen reservations and colonies in Utah, Idaho, Nevada, Wyoming, and California. Many of the reservations are also homes to Arapaho, Bannock, Paiute, and Goshute people.

Today, some Native American tribes still participate in ceremonial festivals called powwows.

The Shoshone built cultural centers (right) to help keep their heritage alive. Some Shoshone used rattles and fans (below) during peyote religious ceremonies.

Religion

Shoshone groups have a wide range of religious practices. Some believe that the sun made the heavens and earth. Others think that a coyote, wolf, or a kindly spirit called "Our Father" created the world. The people seek the help of these and other spirits.

Many Shoshone groups have no priests or other religious leaders. Instead, people connect to supernatural powers on their own through visions and dreams.

Another Shoshone practice is the peyote (pronounced *pay-OH-tee*) religion. It spread throughout North America in the late 19th and early 20th centuries. Many Shoshone saw it as a source of comfort and strength in the face of hardship. Peyote is a type of cactus. When it is chewed, the user may see visions. The Shoshone, who believe in strong links to spirits, think peyote makes it easier to get in touch with supernatural powers.

The Shoshone also welcomed the Ghost Dance religions of 1870 and 1889. Ghost Dancers performed a special dance. It was supposed to help bring back traditional ways of life and to free native peoples from white power.

Government

The Western Shoshone were the most loosely organized group. Their small bands sometimes had headmen with little control. The chiefs of Shoshone buffalo hunters were more likely to have more power. This helped the tribe face its enemies in fights over hunting lands.

For the Eastern Shoshone, chiefs were more important. Older men who had proved their worth in past battles were chosen to lead.

In the 1930s, new federal policies brought self-government to the Shoshone. Today, many reservations and colonies are run by elected tribal and business councils.

Chief Tendoy III (left) was a Shoshone leader in 1927, around the time the tribe was first allowed to practice self-government.

Economy

The Shoshone were hunter-gatherers. What they hunted and gathered was based on where they lived. For example, those who lived near water fished. The Shoshone also traded. They gave the Crow Indians horses in return for metal arrow points. Later, they traded furs to whites for horses and weapons.

In the late 1800s and early 1900s, many Shoshone came to depend on wages paid by white employers. Shoshone on reservations were encouraged to farm, even if the land was not fertile. They faced hardship when government agents did not bring supplies or seeds. By the start of the 21st century, many Shoshone were still poor.

In the late 19th and early 20th centuries, many Shoshone farmed reservation land to make a living.

SHOSHONE POPULATION: 1990 CENSUS

In the 1990 U.S. Census, 9,506 people said they were Shoshone. They identified themselves this way:

Group name	1990 population
Battle Mountain	82
Ely	153
Goshute	209
Shoshone	7,925
Te-Moak Western Shoshone	932
Timbi-Sha Shoshone	47
Washakie	66
Yomba	44
Other Shoshone	48

Source: 1990 census of population and housing. Subject summary tape file (SSTF) 13 (computer file): characteristics of American Indians by tribe and language. Washington, D.C.: U.S. Department of Commerce, Bureau of the Census, Data User Services Division, 1995.

The Eastern Shoshone faced the worst economic troubles. Their reservation is in a rugged, mountainous area. To make money, the people lease land for grazing. Some raise horses and cattle. They earn some income from tourists, who are drawn by

Today, some Shoshone raise cattle on ranches.

the reservation's location near the Rocky Mountains and Yellowstone and Grand Teton National Parks. Many tribal members work in government programs, such as social services.

The Northern Shoshone have fared better. They have opened shops and gambling businesses. They also farm. The tribe grows potatoes, grain, and alfalfa. The people also raise cattle and lease land to other farmers. Still, the tribe suffered when a mine on the reservation closed in 1993.

The Western Shoshone are cattle ranchers. They continue to struggle with the U.S. government over land rights even today.

DAILY LIFE

Buildings

Some Northern Shoshone lived in tepees made from buffalo hides or woven rushes (marsh plants) and willows. Others built cone-shaped homes of brush and grass. All Northern groups built sweat lodges.

The Western Shoshone lived in more permanent camps than other Shoshone groups did. This was because they did not chase the buffalo. For the winter, they built cone-shaped huts with bark walls. Rings of

Some Shoshone made tepees from plants and buffalo hides.

The Northern Shoshone built sweat lodges such as this one.

stone held up the walls. Some built sunshades and circle-shaped cottages out of brush and light timber. Many Western Shoshone lived in wickiups (pronounced *WIK-ee-ups*). These were frame huts covered with brush or bark. Other Shoshone did not build homes at all. They simply looked for shelter in caves when the weather was bad.

The Eastern Shoshone built tepees. Each of these structures used the hides of at least ten buffalo. The chief's tepee might be painted with a yellow band to set it apart from others.

Clothing

Most Shoshone wore few clothes. Women and girls usually wore only skirts and hats. Young boys went naked. When it was very cold, the Shoshone wore dresses, shirts, and robes made from furs and hides. The best hunters had larger garments made from deer and antelope skins.

Buffalo-hunting people wore buffalo robes in winter and elk skins in summer. Leggings and breech-cloths (garments with front and back flaps that hang from the waist) were also common. Those who did not go barefoot wore moccasins of buffalo hide.

Both sexes pierced their ears and wore necklaces. Western Shoshone painted their faces and bodies. Some also had tattoos on their faces.

In cold weather, Shoshone women sometimes wore dresses made from animal hides (left). Shoshone hunters often wore robes made from animal skins, such as buffalo hide.

Food

Shoshone bands were often named for the main foods they ate. Names such as "Salmon Eaters" and "Squirrel Eaters" were common. Some Northern and Eastern Shoshone bands depended on buffalo for most of their food. Men also hunted sheep and antelope. Other Shoshone caught fish. They are said to have used torches to attract fish at night. They then netted or trapped the fish.

Shoshone women made cakes from dried berries, nuts, and seeds. They cooked turnips and other vegetables in pits beneath hot rocks.

The Western Shoshone used sticks to dig up edible plants and nuts. The Western Shoshone hunted small game, such as rabbits and rodents. They also fished and swept through open fields to catch grasshoppers to eat.

The Shoshone relied on animal meat and wild plants for food. Women made cakes from dried berries and seeds.

Education

Elderly and disabled people taught children. They sang songs and told stories while parents looked for food. At the start of the 20th century, Christian missionaries set up boarding schools. Some Shoshone children were sent there, far from their homes. At these schools, children had to speak English. Among the Shoshone, these efforts to end native customs were not very successful.

Shoshone children started to attend public schools in the 1950s.

In the 1950s, Shoshone children began to go to public schools. Test results from the 1990s showed that some Shoshone children lagged behind other students. This may be due to cultural differences. Native students may have trouble with the English language. Little American Indian history and culture are taught in many schools.

Students at the Wind River Reservation have their own Wyoming Indian High School. It teaches native culture and language. Other Shoshone communities run programs for preschoolers.

Shoshone healers helped cure illness using natural materials and spiritual powers.

Healing practices

The Shoshone had men or women healers called shamans (pronounced SHAH-munz or SHAY-munz). These people used plants, charms, and chants to cure illnesses. Shamans got the spirit powers that helped them heal people through visions. The shaman often put hands on the patient or sucked out the disease-causing object.

Government reforms that began in the 1930s brought modern health care. This trend continued through the end of the 20th century. As a result, the Shoshone population grew.

Arts

All Shoshone groups have their own artistic traditions. Once they began to use horses to travel, many groups learned about the art of their neighbors. Several techniques, such as elk- and buffalo-hide painting, were used to record tribal history.

Western Shoshone art is very different from that of the Northern and Eastern groups. Western Shoshone made baskets and tools to carry what little water and food they found. They also had no leather, so they wove willows and grasses into beautiful yet useful items.

The Shoshone painted animal hides to record their history.

Literature

Sacajawea's brother is said to have produced the first written Shoshone story. Shoshone authors have written tribal histories, and newspapers are published at the Wind River and Fort Hall Reservations.

CUSTOMS

Festivals and ceremonies

All Shoshone had several ceremonies. Major dances included the Round Dance, the Father Dance, and the Sun Dance. The Round Dance was done when food was plentiful or as part of a yearly mourning ceremony. The Father Dance honored the Creator and asked for good health. The Sun Dance was done after a buffalo hunt. The head of a buffalo was prepared so that it seemed to be alive. Today, a mounted buffalo head is used. The Sun Dance shows unity and renews ties to spiritual life.

Today, the Shoshone hold fandangos (festivals that include prayers and games) and powwows. The powwow—a traditional song-and-dance celebration—only came to the Shoshone in 1957.

Ceremonial dances, such as the Round Dance, were an important part of Shoshone culture.

COYOTE WANTS TO BE CHIEF

The Shoshone have many tales of Coyote, a trickster who created people. Coyote is a main character in many tales of western tribes.

People from all over the country—all kinds of animals, even Stink Bug—gathered together in a valley for a council. Rumors were going around that a lot of them wanted to make Coyote the head man. Meadowlark told Coyote that Coyote was going to be a great chief. As he was going along, Coyote met Skunk, who told him the same thing, that Coyote was going to be the biggest chief there ever was.

Tales about Coyote, the trickster, were popular among the Shoshone.

Then Coyote met Badger and he said the same thing. Every time Coyote heard this he got so swelled and he wished he would meet some more people who would tell him the same things.

Coyote wanted to find [Wolf] his brother. Wolf had been away for a long time. Coyote ran around that valley

War rituals

The Eastern Shoshone had military societies called the Yellow Brows and the Logs. Yellow Brows went through an interesting initiation ritual. In it, all speech was backward. For example, "yes" so fast, looking for Wolf, that he got all tired out.

The council was to start before the sun came up. Coyote didn't sleep the night before, [so] he was so weary. In the middle of the night Coyote got sleepy. He still had a long way to go to get to the council. Coyote sat down to rest a little while in some timber. He didn't want to go to sleep but he was very weary. His eyes began to close. He picked up some little yellow flowers and propped his eyelids open with them. He fought sleep but he was so tired. Finally he fell asleep and didn't wake up till noon the next day. He got up and ran toward the valley. To his surprise he began meeting people. They were coming back from the council. He started asking, "What did you talk about? Who became a chief?" And they all told him, "Your brother did. He is the biggest man in the country now. He is the chief."

Coyote wanted to find his brother. Then Coyote found his brother and asked him if he were the biggest chief. Wolf said, "Yes." The people all wanted him to be the biggest chief.

SOURCE: Tom Steward, *Shoshone Tales*. Edited by Anne M. Smith. Salt Lake City: University of Utah Press, 1993.

meant "no." The young men painted their hair yellow and promised to be fearless. They vowed not to give up even if they faced certain death. Logs were older soldiers. They painted their faces black.

A Shoshone military society practiced its rituals in Fort Hall, Idaho. Eastern Shoshone had initiation rituals that included changing the way they spoke.

Courtship and marriage

Most couples met at Round Dances. Some men, however, kidnapped their brides—and did not care if the women were single or married. Good hunters were sought as husbands. They often had more than one wife. Divorce was common and people often remarried.

The role of women

In early times, Shoshone women were seen as inferior to men. As women grew older, there were ways to raise their standing in the group. They could heal people, help at births, or show skill at gambling. Shoshone women were respected more by Europeans because they were often go-betweens for trappers and traders.

INDIAN SQUAWS
WEARING ELK TOOTH ROBES.
FT HALL RESERVATION, IDAHO.

Shoshone women (such as those pictured toward front of photo) earned the respect of whites because they served as go-betweens for European trappers and traders.

Death and burial

Some Shoshone wrapped their dead in blankets and placed them in rock crevices. They believed the souls of the dead went to the lands of Coyote or Wolf. Mourners cut their hair and destroyed the dead person's property, horse, and tepee. The ghosts of the dead were feared. It was considered a bad sign even to dream about someone who had died.

Current tribal issues

The Western Shoshone continue to have land claim struggles with the government. They reject offers of money. Instead, they hope to win back some of the 22 million acres they have lost since the 19th century. In 1972, the Shoshone joined with a group called the American Indian Movement (AIM) in a political demonstration. Five hundred Indians went to Washington, D.C., to protest government policies.

In 2002, Western Shoshone protested against the government's proposal to build a nuclear waste facility on a site they believe to be sacred. Land claims are an ongoing concern for the tribe.

Notable people

Chief Washakie signed the Treaty of Fort Bridger in 1863.

Washakie (c. 1804–1900) was a chief of the Eastern Shoshone. In the 1820s and 1830s, Washakie and the Shoshone were on good terms with whites. Washakie signed the Treaty of Fort Bridger in 1863, which promised travelers safe passage through his band's lands. His good relations with the U.S. government helped the Eastern Shoshone get the Wind River Reservation in Wyoming.

Sacajawea (c. 1784–c. 1812) guided explorers Lewis and Clark on their westward journey. She was part of the Lemhi Shoshone of Idaho and Montana.

Around the age of ten, she was kidnapped by the Hidatsa tribe. In 1804, a trader, Toussaint Charbonneau, bought and married her. Charbonneau and Sacajawea joined the Lewis and Clark expedition just before she gave birth to their child. Sacajawea showed the people Lewis and Clark met that their mission was peaceful.

Other notable Shoshone include: Pocatello (c. 1815–1884), who fiercely resisted white settlement; Bear Hunter (d. 1863), who died in a U.S. army raid; and author Laine Thom (1952–), who edited two books about the American Indian experience.

For More Information

Dramer, Kim. *The Shoshone*. Broomall, PA: Chelsea House, 1997.

Trenholm, Virginia Cole, and Maurine Carley. *The Shoshonis: Sentinels of the Rockies*. Norman: University of Oklahoma Press, 1964.

This statue honors Sacajawea, the Shoshone guide who helped the Lewis and Clark expedition. She and her husband, trader Toussaint Charbonneau, joined the explorers right before she gave birth.

Glossary

Epidemic an outbreak of disease that affects many people

Expedition a journey taken for the purpose of discovery or study

Massacre a mass killing of a group of people

Reservation a plot of land set aside by the United States government for Native Americans

Shaman a priest or priestess who uses magic for the purpose of curing the sick, divining the future, and controlling events.

Timber wood

Treaty agreement

Tribe a group of people who live together in a community

Wickiups frame huts covered with brush or bark

Index